About this book

This book is for everyone who is learning their first words in German. By looking at the pictures, it will be easy to read and remember the words underneath.

When you look at the German words, you will see that in front of most of them is **der, die** or **das**, which means "the". When learning German, it is a good idea to learn the **der, die** or **das** which goes with each one. This is because all words, like table and clock, as well as man and woman are masculine or feminine, and some words, like bed, are neuter. **Der** means the word is masculine, **die** means it is feminine, and **das** means it is neuter. **Die** is also the word for "the" before plural words — that is, more than one, like tables or beds.

Most German words begin with a capital, or big, letter unlike most English words. There is also the letter ß in some words which is the same as "ss" written in English. On some vowels — a, o, and u — there are two dots, like this ä, ö, ü. This is called an umlaut and changes the way the vowel is said.

At the back of the book is a guide to help you say all the words in the pictures. But there are some sounds in German which are quite different from any sound in English. To say the German word correctly, you have to hear it said, listen very carefully and then try to say it that way yourself. But if you say a word as it is written in the guide, a German person will understand you, even if your German accent is not quite perfect.

THE FIRST HUNDRED WORDS IN GERMAN

Heather Amery
Illustrated by Stephen Cartwright

Translated by Anita Ganeri

There is a little yellow duck to find in every picture.

Das Wohnzimmer The living room

Vati
Daddy

Mutti
Mommy

der Junge
boy

das Mädchen
girl

das Baby
baby

der Hund
dog

die Katze
cat

Die Kleider Clothes

das Unterhemd
undershirt

die Unterhose
underwear

die Schuhe
shoes

die Socken
socks

die Hose
pants

das T-shirt
T-shirt

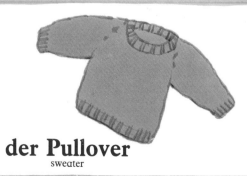

der Pullover
sweater

In der Küche In the kitchen

das Brot
bread

die Milch
milk

die Eier
eggs

der Apfel
apple

die Orange
orange

die Banane
banana

7

Der Abwasch Doing the dishes

der Tisch
table

der Stuhl
chair

der Teller
plate

das Messer
knife

die Gabel
fork

der Löffel
spoon

die Tasse
cup

Das Spielzeug Toys

das Pferd
horse

das Schaf
sheep

die Kuh
cow

das Huhn
hen

das Schwein
pig

der Zug
train

die Bausteine
blocks

Einen Besuch machen Going on a visit

Oma
Grandma

Opa
Grandpa

die Hausschuhe
slippers

das Kleid
dress

der Mantel
coat

die Mütze
hat

Im Park In the park

der Baum
tree

die Blume
flower

die Schaukeln
swings

der Ball
ball

die Rutschbahn
slide

der Vogel
bird

die Stiefel
boots

das Boot
boat

Auf der Straße In the street

das Auto
car

das Fahrrad
bicycle

der Lastwagen
truck

der Bus
bus

das Flugzeug
airplane

das Haus
house

Die Party The party

das Eis
ice cream

der Kuchen
cake

der Ballon
balloon

die Uhr
clock

der Fisch
fish

die Kekse
cookies

die Bonbons
candy

Das Schwimmbad The swimming pool

der Arm arm   **die Hand** hand   **das Bein** leg   **die Füße** feet

die Zehen
toes

der Kopf
head

der Hintern
bottom

Der Umkleideraum The changing room

der Mund
mouth

die Augen
eyes

die Ohren
ears

die Nase
nose

die Haare
hair

der Kamm
comb

die Bürste
brush

Das Geschäft The store

rot
red

blau
blue

grün
green

gelb
yellow

rosa
pink

weiß
white

schwarz
black

Das Badezimmer The bathroom

das Bad
bathtub

das Handtuch
towel

die Toilette
toilet

die Seife
soap

der Bauch
tummy

die Ente
duck

Das Schlafzimmer <small>The bedroom</small>

das Bett
<small>bed</small>

das Fenster
<small>window</small>

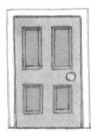

die Tür
<small>door</small>

 **ie Lampe**
light

**das Buch**
book

**die Puppe**
doll

**der Teddy**
teddy

Match the words to the pictures

der Apfel

das Auto

der Ball

die Banane

das Buch

das Ei

das Eis

die Ente

das Fenster

der Fisch

die Gabel

der Hund

die Katze

der Kuchen

die Kuh

die Lampe

das Messer

die Milch

die Mütze

die Orange

der Pullover

die Puppe

das Schwein

die Socken

die Stiefel

der Teddy

der Tisch

die Uhr

das Unterhemd

der Zug

Die Zählung Counting

1 eins one

2 zwei two

3 drei three

4 vier four

5 fünf five

1 eins one **2 zwei** two **3 drei** three **4 vier** four **5 fünf** five

Words in the pictures

In this alphabetical list of the words in the pictures, the German word comes first, next is the guide to saying the word, and then there is the English translation. Although some German words look like English ones, they are not said in the same way. And some letters have different sounds. In German, w sounds like English v, v sounds like f, z like ts, and j like y in yellow. There are also some sounds in German which are quite different from any sound in English.

The guide is to help you say the words correctly. They may look strange or funny but just read them as if they are English words, remembering these special rules:

ah is said like *a* in *farther*
a is said like *a* in *add*
ow is like *ow* in *cow*
e(w) is different from any sound in English. To make it, say *ee* with your lips rounded.
ee is like *ee* in *week*
ay is like *ay* in *day*
y is like *y* in *try*, except when it comes before a vowel. Then it sounds like *y* in *yellow*.
g is like *g* in *garden*
kh is like *ch* in the word *loch* or the *h* in *huge*.
r is rolled at the back of your mouth
er is like *er* in *butter*

German	Guide	English
der Abwasch	*derr abvash*	doing the dishes
der Apfel	*derr apfel*	apple
der Arm	*derr arm*	arm
die Augen	*dee owgen*	eyes
das Auto	*dass owto*	car
das Baby	*dass baby*	baby
das Bad	*dass bahd*	bathtub
das Badezimmer	*dass bahder-tsimmer*	bathroom
der Ball	*derr bal*	ball
der Ballon	*derr ballon*	balloon
die Banane	*dee bananer*	banana
der Bauch	*derr bowkh*	tummy
der Baum	*derr bowm*	tree
die Bausteine	*dee bow-shtine*	blocks
das Bein	*dass bine*	leg
das Bett	*dass bet*	bed
blau	*blaow*	blue
die Blume	*dee bloomer*	flower
die Bonbons	*dee bonbons*	candy
das Boot	*dass boat*	boat
das Brot	*dass broat*	bread
das Buch	*dass bookh*	book
die Bürste	*dee bewrster*	brush
der Bus	*derr booss*	bus
drei	*dry*	three
das Ei	*dass eye*	egg
die Eier	*dee eyer*	eggs
eins	*ynss*	one
das Eis	*dass ice*	ice cream
die Ente	*dee enter*	duck
das Fahrrad	*dass fahr-raht*	bicycle
das Fenster	*dass fenster*	window
der Fisch	*derr fish*	fish
das Flugzeug	*dass floog-tsoyk*	airplane
fünf	*fewnf*	five
die Füße	*dee fooser*	feet
die Gabel	*dee gahbel*	fork
gelb	*gelp*	yellow
das Geschäft	*dass gay-sheft*	store
grün	*grewn*	green
die Haare	*dee hahrer*	hair
die Hand	*dee hant*	hand
das Handtuch	*dass hant-tookh*	towel
das Haus	*dass house*	house
die Hausschuhe	*dee house-shooer*	slippers
der Hintern	*derr hintern*	bottom
die Hose	*dee hoze*	pants

German	Pronunciation	English
das Huhn	dass hoon	hen
der Hund	derr hoont	dog
der Junge	derr yoonger	boy
der Kamm	derr kamm	comb
die Katze	dee katser	cat
die Kekse	dee kekser	biscuits
das Kleid	dass klyt	dress
die Kleider	dee klyder	clothes
der Kopf	derr kopf	head
die Küche	dee kewkher	kitchen
der Kuchen	derr kookhen	cake
die Kuh	dee koo	cow
die Lampe	dee lamper	light
der Lastwagen	derr last-vahgen	truck
der Löffel	derr lurfel	spoon
das Mädchen	dass mayt-khen	girl
der Mantel	derr mantel	coat
das Messer	dass messer	knife
die Milch	dee milkh	milk
der Mund	derr moont	mouth
Mutti	mootee	Mummy
die Mütze	dee mewtze(r)	hat
die Nase	dee nahzer	nose
die Ohren	dee oren	ears
Oma	ohmar	Granny
Opa	ohpar	Grandpa
die Orange	dee oranjer	orange
der Park	derr park	park
die Party	dee party	party
das Pferd	dass pfert	horse
der Pullover	derr pool-ofer	jumper
die Puppe	dee pooper	doll
rosa	roza	pink
rot	roat	red
die Rutschbahn	dee rootsch-bahn	slide
das Schaf	dass shahf	sheep
die Schaukeln	dee showkeln	swings
das Schlafzimmer	dass schlarf-tsimmer	bedroom
die Schuhe	dee shooer	shoes
schwarz	shvarts	black
das Schwein	dass shvine	pig
das Schwimmbad	dass schvim-bahd	swimming pool
die Seife	dee zyfer	soap
die Socken	dee zocken	socks
das Spielzeug	dass shpeel-tsoyk	toys
die Stiefel	dee shteefel	boots
die Straße	dee shtrasser	street
der Stuhl	derr shtool	chair
die Tasse	dee tasser	cup
der Teddy	derr teddy	teddy
der Teller	derr teller	plate
der Tisch	derr tish	table
die Toilette	dee twaletter	toilet
das T-shirt	dass tee-shirt	T-shirt
die Tür	dee tewr	door
die Uhr	dee oor	clock
der Umkleideraum	der oom-klider-rowm	changing room
das Unterhemd	dass oonter-hemt	vest
die Unterhose	dee oonter-hoser	pants
Vati	fartee	Daddy
vier	feer	four
der Vogel	derr fogel	bird
weiß	vyss	white
die Wohnzimmer	dee vone-tsimmer	living room
die Zählung	dee tsahl-oong	counting
die Zehen	dee tsayen	toes
der Zug	derr tsook	train
zwei	tsvy	two